Black Wall Street: The History of the Greenwood District Before the Tulsa Race Riot

By Charles River Editors

Charles River Editors is a boutique digital publishing company, specializing in bringing history back to life with educational and engaging books on a wide range of topics. Keep up to date with our new and free offerings with this 5 second sign up on our weekly mailing list, and visit Our Kindle Author Page to see other recently published Kindle titles.

We make these books for you and always want to know our readers' opinions, so we encourage you to leave reviews and look forward to publishing new and exciting titles each week.

Introduction

   In the wake of the Civil War, African Americans attained freedom from chattel slavery, but continued to suffer discrimination both legal in the form of Jim Crow laws and de facto in the continued perception among the vast majority of white Americans that African Americans were at the very least inferior and at the most a constant dangerous presence in their communities who must be carefully controlled. In this way, Tulsa was no different than most cities in the region in the 1920s.

   Overall, Tulsa in 1921 was considered a modern, vibrant city. What had fueled this remarkable growth was oil, specifically the discovery of the Glenn Pool oil field in 1905. Within five years, Tulsa had grown from a rural crossroads town in the former Indian Territory into a boomtown with more than 10,000 citizens, and as word spread of the fortunes that could be made in Tulsa, people of all races poured into the city. By 1920, the greater Tulsa area boasted a population of over 100,000. In turn, Tulsa's residential neighborhoods were some of the most modern and stylish in the country, and the Tulsa Chamber of Commerce produced postcards and literature boasting of the virtues of life in their modern oil city. However, as a commission report about the Tulsa Riot later pointed out, "What the pamphlets and the picture postcards did not reveal was that, despite of its impressive new architecture and its increasingly urbane affectations, Tulsa was a deeply troubled town. As 1920 turned into 1921, the city would soon face a crossroads that, in the end, would change it forever...Tulsa was, in some ways, not one city but two."

  When they came to Tulsa, many blacks settled in the Greenwood area and established a thriving commercial, cultural, and residential area. Of course, the segregation was forced on these residents, and while they had fled the worst conditions of the Jim Crow South in other areas, they were not able to escape it completely. But in one way, Tulsa was different for African Americans, as black citizens of the city shared in the city's wealth, albeit not as equally as their white neighbors. The Greenwood district, a 36 square block section of northern Tulsa, was considered the wealthiest African American neighborhood in the country, called the "Black Wall Street" because of the large number of affluent and professional residents. In the 2001 final report of the Oklahoma Commission to Study the Tulsa Race Riot of 1921, historians John Hope Franklin and Scott Ellsworth described the Greenwood area that would be all but destroyed in one of America's most notorious riots: "In less than twenty-four hours, nearly all of Tulsa's African-American residential district--some forty-square-blocks in all--had been laid to waste, leaving nearly nine-thousand people homeless. Gone, too, was the city's African American commercial district, a thriving area located among Greenwood Avenue which boasted some of the finest black-owned businesses in the Southwest. The Stradford Hotel, a modern fifty-four room brick establishment which housed a drug store, barber shop, restaurant and banquet hall, had been burned to the ground. So had the Gurley Hotel, the Red Wing Hotel, and the Midway Hotel. Literally dozens of family-run businesses--from cafes and mom-and-pop grocery stores, to the Dreamland Theater, the Y.M.C.A. cleaners, the East End Feed Store, and Osborne Monroe's roller skating rink--had also gone up in flames, taking with them the livelihoods, and in many cases the life savings, of literally hundreds of people. The offices of two newspapers--the *Tulsa Star* and the *Oklahoma Sun*-- had also been destroyed, as were the offices of more than a dozen doctors, dentists, lawyers, realtors, and other professionals. A United States Post Office substation was

burned as was the all-black Frissell Memorial Hospital.
The brand new Booker T. Washington High School
building escaped the torches of the rioters, but Dunbar
Elementary School did not. Neither did more than a half
dozen African-American churches, including the newly
constructed Mount Zion Baptist Church, an impressive
brick tabernacle which had been dedicated only seven
weeks earlier."

Tragically, the decades following the riot saw the
memory of it recede into the background. The *Tulsa
Tribune* did not recognize the riot in its "Fifteen Years
Ago Today" or "Twenty-five Years Ago Today" features.
In 1971, the Tulsa Chamber of Commerce decided to
commemorate the riot, but when they read the materials
gathered by Ed Wheeler about the riot, they refused to
publish any of it, and the Tulsa papers also refused to run
Wheeler's story. He finally published an article in a black
magazine, *Impact Magazine*; but most of Tulsa's white
citizens never knew about it. It would not be until recently
that a true accounting of the riot and its damage have been
conducted, and as the 100th anniversary of the massacre
approaches in 2021, the city of Tulsa is still working to
complete the historical record.

*Black Wall Street: The History of the Greenwood
District Before the Tulsa Race Riot* examines the
conditions and events that led to the rise of the district and

what life was like there. Along with pictures depicting important people, places, and events, you will learn about Black Wall Street like never before.

Black Wall Street: The History of the Greenwood District Before the Tulsa Race Riot

About Charles River Editors

Introduction

Before the Rise of Black Wall Street

Tulsa

The Rise of Black Wall Street

Unrest

Greenwood's Legacy

Online Resources

Bibliography

Free Books by Charles River Editors

Discounted Books by Charles River Editors

Before the Rise of Black Wall Street

The historical quest for economic prosperity among non-white cultures in the United States was dealt a nearly unplayable hand from the country's founding. African Americans, who built much of the nation's infrastructure through its first century of existence, had no ancestral access to western wealth, lived under a status scarcely above that ascribed to beasts of burden, and found few champions outside their own culture. A stolen and enslaved people, efforts to demonstrate equal intelligence, worthiness of education, aspirations toward tangible success, and the drive to prosper was counterproductive to a white system dependent on their continued subjugation.

The "emancipation" granted by Lincoln's Emancipation Proclamation signaled a technical status of freedom for the slave, but it did not in any sense guarantee social equality. After all, such a status lies beyond the power of legislation if the dominant culture would not tolerate or otherwise embrace the idea. Every pursuit of employment began with a racial disadvantage, and the Jim Crow laws in the South effectively reinstated a constraint on much of the slaves' range of movement, opportunity, and right to civic participation.

By the approach of the 20th century two strategies had come to the forefront for black advancement. Booker T.

Washington envisioned a rise in his culture's former slave status by developing a general usefulness in what would now be known as blue-collar labor or basic agricultural skills. However, for W.E.B. Du Bois, the underlying equation of subservience was unaltered as his race moved from slave labor to poorly paid lackeys at the lowest levels of white business. Du Bois exhorted the African American to stand and declare his right to prosperity, education, and status within an economic system predisposed to shutting him out. Either way, positions of leadership and the time of middle and upper-tier wage earning was far off. However, in a phenomenon scantily taught in secondary education of the twenty-first century, African America gained its footing with a third approach that in developmental terms combined the Washington and Du Bois models.

Washington

Du Bois

The alteration from a standard habit of begging or demanding status from a race for which equality was counterproductive was to be found in cultural and physical isolation, entrepreneurship, self-help and internally generated profit. Black business interests managed to rid themselves of white hierarchy in a few spots on the east coast and in the Midwest. Land was bought and sold exclusively within the black community, and the currency generated remained in the black system. All kinds of businesses were established in mono-racial enclaves with assistance from black lending institutions devoted to increased opportunity for African American success.

The most notable example of these black *Camelots* - organized, efficient, wealthy and collaborative - rose out of the city of Tulsa, Oklahoma on hostile ground where the black man occupied the lowest rung of civil rights. Hundreds of businesses ranging from the essential to the luxurious effectively debunked white stereotypes of African American laziness, mental deficiency, immorality, and general shiftlessness. White Tulsans looked on while their neighbors, the children of slaves, met or outpaced their standard of living. A culture that was once forbidden to receive basic literacy now sent their children to institutions such as Columbia University, Tuskegee Institute under the guidance of Washington, Howard University, and Spelman College.

Indeed, what was to become hailed as "Black Wall Street" in the enclave of the Greenwood District led the region in high-level financing and demonstrated sophisticated investment skills that outpaced the city norm. The school system became a model of success, and residents bought fine homes, maintained an opulent social life, and became patrons of the arts. Naturally, former slaves had always desired access to the same opportunities and possessions of their masters, along with the freedom to employ them at will. The secret seemed to be found in constructive segregation, living apart and asking nothing from a resentful outside world whose objective it was to leave the black community in debt.

The Greenwood District of Tulsa was not the only example of socioeconomic triumph created by the first generation that followed emancipation. The Jackson Ward of Richmond, Virginia became the "epicenter of black banking"[1] in the otherwise rigid environment of Jim Crow prevalent in other sections of the city. Hayti, North Carolina, named for the Caribbean island nation of Haiti, prospered amidst the population of Durham. Freedmen had come to work in the tobacco warehouses, and in time created North Carolina Life Insurance, the wealthiest black-owned company in the state. The administrators added all manner of land development, including a self-sufficient hospital staffed with black doctors and nurses. By the first decade of the 20th century, a library, theater, and 200 retail businesses had been added. Similar examples could be found in the "Little Harlem" of Birmingham, Alabama, Marcus Garvey's Harlem in New York City, and in the following decades, Boley, Oklahoma.

The establishment of black prosperity in Tulsa came about as the culmination of several factors, the first being the destruction of the American South. Both the land and aristocratic life within the plantation culture were

---

[1] Michael Harriot, The Other Black Wall Streets, The Root – www.theroot.com, the-other-black-wall-streets-1823010812

shattered, and with a sporadic industrial capacity, recovery proceeded at a snail's pace. The post-civil war years comprised an era of migrations, from Native American relocations to blacks seeking escape from Jim Crow. Lincoln could speak all he liked of emancipation, but he could not alter the caste system of the South. The white overlord was determined to retain his liberated black labor force under an alternate set of legal restraints.

The great bulk of the American South, barren and unproductive after the sweeping Union invasions, was unkind to the farmers above all others.. Eking out a bare existence for black sharecroppers left them constantly on the borders of bankruptcy and starvation. In order to approximate the pre-war status of slaves and to keep in place old traditions of behavior and financial struggle among the newly emancipated, the Democratic Party established Jim Crow to sustain white supremacy in the region. The concept consisted of a tangle of state and local statutes controlling black behavior, named after a minstrel show character of the time, and these extreme legislations endured for decades, keeping black America legally subjugated past the mid-20th century. Jim Crow maintained a state of segregation, suppressed the rights of non-whites to vote, barred access to a formal education, and set a strict code of public behavior. To understand the code was paramount, and violating it was perilous to one's safety. Black residents could not go certain places in white communities, could not freely seek employment above their station, and could not bargain freely for wages. Blacks in financial arrears were attached to families as indentured servants, and children of any age could be seized for labor or collateral. The code was not only instituted to maintain dominance over black residents, but for the poor of any color.

The code was overseen by former Confederate soldiers who took up positions as post-war police officers, judges, and politicians, and behind the entire phenomenon loomed the Ku Klux Klan, a terrorist group keeping non-whites in line through acts of violence and intimidation. The KKK was established at the war's end in Pulaski, Tennessee as a private club for former Confederate officers. Some suggest that the "white hood brigade"[2] was initiated by Confederate General Nathan Bedford Forrest, who viewed blacks as human beings rather than statistics and "troublemakers."[3] Forrest apparently severed his association with the first chapter after "undesirables"[4] perverted the group's ideals.

According to Glenda Gilmore of Yale University, the stranglehold Jim Crow exerted on the South was

---

[2] Jerry Bowyer, Tulsa Massacre: The Loser Class vs. Black Entrepreneurs, Townhall Finance, June 23, 2020 – www.finance.townhall.com/columnists/jerrybowyer/2020/06/23/tulsa-massacre-the-loser-class-vs-black-entrepreneurs-n2571165

[3] Oklahoma Historical Society, Ku Klux Klan-www.okhistory.org/publications/enc/entry.php?entry=KU001

[4] Oklahoma Historical Society

malleable as black residents and white sympathizers explored new methods of resistance, requiring the system to "prove its power"[5] on a regular basis. The code was forced to rebrand and re-legislate itself as politicians struggled to retain their grip. With enough support from outside the black population, its power was never "complete or total." Thus, in the end, the Southern black sharecroppers who were financially clear of servitude but bound to a marginal existence held one ace – to pack what little they had and leave for better places with less abusive histories.

As a result, even as freedom from slavery represented a "radical transformation"[6] for the African American population, despite the change in technical and legal status as citizens, the economic and demographic realities were not so significantly altered. According to the 1890 Census, 90% of blacks still lived in the South, roughly the same percentage as 20 years prior. Three quarters of the black population was located in rural areas, and less than one half owned their own home. Whites owned their homes at twice that rate, and half of all black men and 35% of black women were either farmers or farm laborers, a vastly higher percentage than that of the white population. African Americans were largely consigned to

---

[5] Glenda Gilmore, Jumpin' Jim Crow: Southern Politics from Civil War to Civil Rights, Department of African American Studies, Yale University – www.afamstudies.yale.edu/publications/jumpin'-him-crow-Southern-politics-civil-war-civil-rights

[6] Thomas N. Maloney, University of Utah, African Americans in the 20th Century, E.H. Net – www.eh.net/encyclopedia/African Americans-in-the-20th-century

unskilled positions, and the percentage of children attending school was far lower than it was for white families. The style of life for blacks was largely a continuation of the past century, taken up with cotton agriculture. Some were part-time laborers while others worked as tenant farmers, renting the land and tools out of an already meager income. Wages between whites and blacks were similar for agricultural work, but white workers were far more likely to own land. They continued to hold higher-skill jobs, while blacks generally worked for lower-wage companies.

In conjunction, the laws against personal rights grew more severe than in the years prior to the Civil War. The Supreme Court's decision in *Plessy v. Ferguson* gave way to an ever-increasing state of segregation and allowed for separate facilities and services between the races. "Separate but equal" was the proposition sold to the black community, which was interesting and paradoxical since black-ordered segregation was to become the bedrock of financial success. Jim Crow laws segregated the schools, all manner of public transportation, lodgings, and government buildings. The accompanying requirement for equal treatment in this divided society was seldom enforced. As an example, money was regularly diverted from the black school systems and funneled into white schools. White teacher salaries rose on a per-pupil basis, while black schools fell into a sharp decline.

By the second decade of the 20th century, the South was altered by a massive northward migration of black workers, causing a four percent drop in the black population over the period of just a few years. The northward movement was in every way tied to either economic circumstances and/or fear of the KKK. Many Northern employers in several industries were experiencing an increased demand for their products and thus required a larger and immediate labor force. The traditional source of labor, immigrants from Europe, dried up due to World War I, while the international flow of immigrant workers was interrupted and worsened by the passage of harsher anti-immigration laws. Turning to African American labor, employers sent recruiters into the South, raising the prospect of a higher wage than the Southern employers could provide and offering to pay each man's way to the factory's location. The North also looked all the better as the boll weevil and weather abnormalities wreaked havoc with the cotton crop. Although black America did not rise out of the unskilled category, the pay was significantly better, and the fields of opportunity were vastly broader.

Of course, there were drawbacks to moving north. Admittance to certain firms could not be procured by black citizens, especially new Southern arrivals. The Ford

Motor Company hired many, but other major automakers in Detroit would not, and in many cases, blacks took on unpleasant and dangerous tasks shunned by some white workers. These included work in meat packing plants, foundry departments of auto companies, and blast furnaces in the production of steel. As unions gained strength in the North, their relationship with the new black workers was often "antagonistic."[7] Most passed explicit rules barring entry to black laborers. When faced with strikes, employers frequently hired black workers as strike-breakers. Black females found the pursuit of work a more difficult proposition as competition grew increasingly "heated"[8] among domestic workers.

Tulsa

Among the possible areas where a higher quality lifestyle was possible, the Oklahoma Territory ended up being a prime arrival point for those who chose to move west instead of north. Created only a year after the war's end, the pursuit of Oklahoma land came about through a request to the federal government to reduce Cheyenne, Comanche, and Arapaho lands, and once accomplished, the region was prepared for a land "rush," in which both whites and blacks were eligible for the pursuit of new acreage. The availability of land in the Oklahoma

[7] Thomas N. Maloney

[8] Oklahoma Historical Society

Territory was made possible by an earlier forced migration of Native Americans from the states of Georgia, Tennessee, Alabama, North Carolina, and Florida. Three decades before the Civil War, Andrew Jackson established the *Indian Removal Act* and sent native landowners on a forced march of 5,043 miles that wound through nine states, now referred to as the "Trail of Tears." Those thrown off their land walked the distance in double file, "many bound in chains."[9] Thousands died reaching what the government called the "Indian colonization zone" at the western edge of the Midwest.

 For purposes of eventual statehood, native land was in perpetuity easy to redraw or reduce, depending on the perceived need, and people took advantage of the confiscated lands from the relocation. However, the generally unknown reality of the Trail of Tears is that the "Five Civilized Tribes," including the Cherokee, Choctaw, Chickasaw, Creek, and Seminole, brought their own black slaves on the forced march, and some of them went on to become crucial in the development of the Greenwood District. A number of the native leaders had acquired extraordinary wealth before taking the journey, such as half Scottish Chief John Ross, leader of the Cherokee Nation. Other wealthy colleagues joined him. A modern perception that one American president put the

---

[9] History.com, The Trail of Tears, Feb. 21, 2020 – www.history.com/topics/native-american-history/trail-of-tears

entire incident into motion is incorrect. The idea of native relocation spanned the administration of nine presidents, and removing them from the South and East was a "popularly endorsed, congressionally sanctioned"[10] scheme. Many speculated that in time, black slaves and their native masters would unite against white domination, but that never occurred. Among those who accompanied natives, most blacks were taken captive as stolen slaves, but there were a small number of freedmen, and a few hundred ran away from their Southern masters and sought haven with the tribes once having arrived in Oklahoma. They were welcomed at first as free people and often adopted as family members, but in time the tribes began purchasing them from the standard American slave markets. , and the Five Civilized Tribes were "deeply committed"[11] to slavery. Before the Civil War, blacks had already joined the tribe in numbers, and the Cherokee brought 1,500 to Oklahoma. The Creek Nation included 300 blacks, and approximately 1,200 were owned by the Chickasaw. Eventually, 8,000 black people were present among the tribes, and throughout this time, native leaders participated in a global economy driven by cotton. They believed without hesitation that they were equal to whites and superior to blacks.

---

[10] Ryan P. Smith how Native American Slaveholders Complicate the Trail of Tears Narrative, Smithsonian Magazine – www.smithsonianmag.com/Smithsonian-institution/how-native-american-slaveholders-complicate-the-trail-of-tears-narrative

[11] Ryan P. Smith

The slaves who eventually reached the Greenwood District as citizens arrived through various diplomatic avenues, and rules governing slavery differed from tribe to tribe. As larger numbers of black refugees from the South arrived, the equation changed. Eventually, the Five Civilized Tribes were forced to accept land allotments in order to remain legal residents of the new state, and while the Dawes Act finalized federal control over Indian land, in a real sense the Native American population transported with their black slaves were the true founders of the city of Tulsa. Unlike emancipated slaves, tribal members were allowed to "own land, vote, and serve on juries"[12] in local judicial systems. After proving their "civility" to the federal government, they were allowed to participate in the social life of a nation that had once counted them as the statistical fraction of a human being regarding public transactions and legislative agendas.

Initially, Southern blacks saw the area as a possibility for the creation of towns and colonies in which they could experience their political rights without interference from Southern oppression. They were enticed to the region by figures such as Edwin McCabe, once the most powerful black man in Kansas. A politician and businessman, McCabe was largely responsible for the black settlement of the Oklahoma Territory. Born in Troy, New York, he

12 Alaina E. Roberts, Assistant Professor, University of Pittsburgh, Commemorating the Tulsa Massacre: A Search for Identity and Historical Complexity, June 4, 2020 – www.ncph.org/history-at-work/commemorating-tulsa-massacre/

served as a clerk on Wall Street before settling in the black town of Nicodemus, Kansas. Making his mark as an attorney, he ran successfully as the Republican candidate for State Auditor. As a speculator, he realized that Oklahoma could serve as a "haven from racism"[13] and be personally profitable. McCabe arrived at the future site of Langston, Oklahoma, a decade before the turn of the century, and established the *Langston City Herald*. The smaller enterprise was to serve as a prototype for the model that reached its culmination in Greenwood. Owning the bulk of available lots, his advertisements in the *Herald* declared the region to be "the paradise of Eden and the garden of the Gods."[14] He added a special draw for Southern blacks suffering under segregation and lynch laws. The advertisement read, "Here the negro can rest from mob law, here he can be secure from every ill of the Southern policies."[15]

These offers of land were strewn through Kansas, Arkansas, Texas, Louisiana, Missouri, and Tennessee, and by 1891, 200 Southern refugees lived in Langston City, including a doctor, minister, and schoolteacher. Soon after, thousands of African Americans arrived in time to participate in the "rush" for land, a brutal race employing whatever mode of transportation one could find. Most

---

[13] Black Past, Edward P. McCabe (1850-1920) – www.blackpast.org/African American-history/maccabe-edwin-p-1850-1920/

[14] Immotionaaame.org

[15] Immotionaame.org

were ready to secure a home for themselves and their families "at any price."[16] Racing through former Native American lands, they staked claims of 1.5 million acres in the Cherokee Strip, valued at $11 million in modern currency. By the start of the 1910s, the farming land had lost its crop price value, and many of the new residents were drawn to the cities.

E. P. M'CABE.

McCabe

After purchasing 320 acres himself, McCabe nearly singlehandedly established the new town, naming it for a

---

[16] Immotionaame.org

recently elected black Congressman. He hoped that the number of black settlers would in time propel him into the governor's office by the time of statehood. However, these dreams fell short when the new state adopted Jim Crow statutes and segregated public transportation. McCabe sold his house to fight the new laws, but the U.S. Supreme Court upheld the state's legislature. He died a deeply disappointed and relatively impoverished man in Chicago during the peak of the coming financial empire in the Greenwood District of Tulsa.

All in all, during the bulk of the great migration from the South, approximately 6 million African Americans relocated. They were pushed even harder by the Ku Klux Klan, despite the fact the KKK had been officially dissolved only four years after the war. Klan members continued to operate underground with the same effectiveness to which they had become accustomed. Despite the terror perpetrated against blacks, the migration dismayed residents of the South. First, they had lost the war despite recapturing the services of its black citizens. Then, they lost the labor force that farmed their fields and built the bulk of their infrastructure.

The African American migration from the farmland produced a total of 32 all-black communities, of which Boley was the most active. Founded by two white entrepreneurs who hired a black man named Tom Haynes to promote the venture, Boley became an even more advanced financial model for the region. In 1905, Booker T. Washington visited and wrote glowingly of the breakthroughs he witnessed, all created by former Southern sharecroppers.

In 1907, Oklahoma achieved statehood. For the white population, the entrance into the union was a boon, but far less so for the black newcomers. The political makeup differed greatly from the modern day. The Republican Party was the liberal force in the expanding U.S., while the Democratic Party housed the Southern plantation families and Jim Crow devotees, and the latter won out in mapping the political fortunes of the new state. New legislation "quickly disenfranchised"[17] black voters and segregated the state school systems along with various other accommodations, creating a resemblance to Southern conditions.

Much of the impetus behind the rigid legislation came from notorious white supremacist Bill "Alfalfa" Murray. In his colorful career, he ran for many state and national offices, with a term as governor and Congressman, adding a later run for President. A Texan, his nickname came from a propensity to promote alfalfa as a crop. Unable to speak publicly without racial slurs, he was considered "something of a clown,"[18] but unfortunately for African

---

[17] Immotionaame.org

Americans of the state, his message of racial warfare was timely, in step with the white voting base of his time. Soon, Jim Crow was as much a part of Oklahoma society as it had been in the Deep South, and the Klan, as it had elsewhere, also arrived.

Murray

Some of the newcomers lost heart and went elsewhere,

[18] William W. Savage, Jr., History is Clear: Alfalfa Bill Murray was a Terrible Bigot, Thursday, June 18, 2020, Non Doc.com – www.nondoc.com/2020/06/18/alfalfa-bill-murray-was-a-terrible-bigot/

"disillusioned."[19] A fair-sized group went further north into Alberta, Canada. Others joined the "Back to Africa"[20] movement. A few hundred even joined the ill-fated Chief Sam expedition. Alfred C. "Chief" Sam, a self-declared African chief, purchased an aging freighter, sold berths, and took a boatload of returnees to Africa. They suffered investigations, deprivation, and were rerouted. Only a few reached Ghana to be warmly welcomed. Others dispersed to varied outcomes, and a second wave of passengers lost all they had when Sam sold the ship, stranding hundreds. Still others went south to Mexico.

All the while, racism limited the growth of some towns, as white residents signed oaths never to "rent, sell, or lease land within Okfuskee County to any person of Negro blood."[21] Thus, as local blacks departed, they left behind a withered tax base putting the towns in financial jeopardy. However, such was not the case in the Greenwood District of Tulsa, where several financial stars came together in an atmosphere of mutual assistance to create the best of the all-black cultures in the Oklahoma region. Already a wealthy area from the discovery of oil, the Greenwood District made sure that they would be included in the feast by controlling their own money in every step of the process.

[19] Oklahoma Historical Society, All-Black Town – www.oklahomahistory.org/publications/end/entry-php?entry=AL009
[20] Oklahoma Historical Society
[21] Oklahoma Historical Society

According to the City Directory of Tulsa, 126 oil companies were operational in and around the city by the first years of the 20th century, and in the following decade, 11,000 black Tulsans would come to reside in the area. Not all of the oil barons who raised Tulsa from the prairie were white. For example, Jake Simmons, Jr. became the leading black entrepreneur in the entire oil industry despite his relatively late arrival in Greenwood. Among the recent immigrants of lesser wealth who came before, many were from Missouri. A large number of freedmen had for years lived in the region, many with the Five Civilized Tribes. As the most illustrious of all the midwestern black enclaves, the Greenwood District lived up to the promise inherent in McCabe's efforts in Langston. Established in the year before official Oklahoma statehood, the "venerable"[22] enclave soon housed a population of 10,000 and served as the most active and affluent entity of African American business and culture in the nation. The single street around which the entire enterprise functioned was Greenwood Avenue, in particular where it intersected with Archer Street.

---

[22] Alexis Clark, Tulsa's "Black Wall Street" Flourished as a Self-Contained Hub in Early 1900s, History.com – www.history.com/news/black-wall-street-tulsa-race-massacre

Simmons, Jr.

Interestingly enough, the broad central avenue was the only major thoroughfare that did not cross the tracks into virtually all-white Tulsa, and the intersection of Greenwood and Archer housed the headquarters of the project. Occupying and developing a larger share of Native American land, some of the black residents transferred from native ownership, while the tribes followed a varied set of rules governing the circumstances under which servants could be released.

What some called "Deep Greenwood,"[23] created by a disciplined organizational process while paralleling rapid population expansion, left "a minimum of order in its

---

[23] Thomas F. Armstrong, Review of Scott Ellsworth's Death in a Promised Land, the Tulsa Race Riot of 1921, *Reviews in American History* Vol. 11 no. 1 (March1983) Johns Hopkins University Press

wake."[24] Corrupt practices on the part of police, as well as political and physical assaults by oilmen against the interests of their competitors, complicated the process, although the danger was somewhat minimized through insular living. Vigilante groups such as the Knights of Liberty wreaked havoc with the Greenwood contingent of International Workers of the World, an international labor union associated with socialism and anarchism. Communist movements have historically sought to turn black populations against societies that once enslaved them, and the Knights of Liberty likely feared that the black population of Greenwood, savvy as it was in the practice of capitalism, may be influenced as such. In the infamous "Tulsa Outrage," a district judge handed over 17 IWW workers to the Knights. They were driven to a desolate location west of town and held at gunpoint. Each victim was bound to a tree, tortured, then tarred and feathered. Their clothes were burned.

Throughout this time, Greenwood continued in its profitable way. Black prairie towns popped up after the Dawes Act allowed the federal government to partition the acreage owned by natives into individual plots, anathema to many tribal members of nomadic and far-ranging populations. However, only those who accepted the partitions were allowed citizenship, and over 90

[24] Thomas F. Armstrong

million acres of tribal land were stripped from the original recipients in the end, given instead to non-natives, both white and black. Black purchasers were eager to amass real estate, and and the Greenwood District of Tulsa became the premiere example of it. Nowhere else had "so many African American men and women come together to create, occupy, and govern their own communities."[25] So heady was the experience that some envisioned a widespread black political bloc, while others imagined a black state in the heart of America.

The Rise of Black Wall Street

Among the dynamic figures who created the Greenwood District's 35 square blocks was Ottawa W. Gurley, a wealthy landowner from the Deep South. Born in Huntsville, Alabama to freed slaves, he grew up in Pine Bluff, Arkansas. Largely self-educated, he married childhood sweetheart Emma, a teacher. Gurley was serving in a "cushy" position with the federal Postal Service during the Grover Cleveland administration, but resigned to participate in the Oklahoma Land Rush two decades before the *Dawes Act* opened the door to black settlers. Gurley risked his entire fortune on the move. When the moment came, O.W. and Emma raced amidst the maniacal "stampede"[26] and found their spot of choice

---

[25] Oklahoma Historical Society

[26] Antoine Gara, The Bezos of Black Wall Street, Forbes – www.forbes.com/peter/antoinegara/2020/06/18the-bezos-of-black-wall-street-tulsa-race-riots-1921/#5b37f7c7f321

after a hysterical 50-mile ride. Their property claim was to become the community of Perry, Oklahoma, one of the territory's new black towns.

Gurley

A driven person of seemingly limitless energy, Gurley ran for County Treasurer and served as the principal of the local school. In the same period, he opened a general store. However, some part of him remained unsatisfied as he heard rumors of "giant oil fields"[27] creating great wealth in Tulsa, 80 miles away. Moving to the larger city that year, where black land ownership was still a curiosity, he pursued his profession as both educator and real estate entrepreneur. Without hesitation, he purchased his first

---

[27] Antoine Gara

large tracts intended for both businesses and residences.

Before the advent of statehood, Gurley's agenda ran headlong into the new state government's first piece of legislation, Senate Bill #1. This act prevented black residents from residing, traveling, and marrying"[28] outside of their race. Also known as the "coach law,"[29] the penalty for a violation ranged from $100-$1000. Two Republicans voted against the Act, supporting the law but in an emergency bill. They objected to the permission of black doctors and nurses to enter white railroad cars, even in an emergency.

The lines of Gurley's newly purchased property ran from Pine Street in the north to the Frisco Railroad tracks to the south, Lansing Avenue in the east to Cincinnati Avenue at the western end. His first business was a rooming house on a dusty trail near the Frisco tracks. Gurley himself named the road Greenwood Ave. in honor of the city in Mississippi. The boarding house was to become popular for blacks escaping the oppression of Mississippi, arriving by train on a regular basis, and the district's moniker was perhaps intended to present a new version of the Southern locale. The black community created by his efforts was the best of the all-black communities in the country since the years of the Civil War. Although Oklahoma housed

---

[28] Black Wall Street.org

[29] Oklahoma Historical Society, Senate Bill One – okhistory.com/publications/enc/entry/php?entry=SE017

nearly all of them, the difference between Greenwood and its contemporary communities was that persecution of black residents was a distant reality, virtually non-existent.

Gurley went on to build three two-story buildings and five residences, purchasing another 80 acres of farmland in Rogers County. In addition, he founded what is now known as the Vernon African Methodist Episcopal Church. The racial climate rendered black residents unable to shop anywhere but Greenwood, a reality that only served to expand the district more quickly. By 1913, many more businesses had become established with the financial help of the city's most prominent bankers. These included the law offices of Buck Colbert Franklin and of physician A.C. Jackson. Two schools appeared, Dunbar and Booker T. Washington High School. The educational system was excellent by any comparison with the rest of the state. Freshmen studied algebra, Latin, and ancient history along with English, science, and music. Sophomores studied economics and geometry. For juniors, the curriculum emphasized trade-oriented subjects. Seniors studied physics and trigonometry, vocal music, art, and bookkeeping. So important was the educational component of the district that teachers were among the most highly paid workers. Many had Steinway pianos in their apartments, considered by much of the world as the king of pianos at the equivalent price of a luxury car or small home.

The Mount Zion Baptist Church took its place next to the Vernon AME to accommodate the enormous Southern Baptist denomination. At its full state of development, the Greenwood district came to house 22 churches. Ricketts' Restaurant became a landmark for dining out and the first Dreamland Theater was constructed by the Williams family within easy reach of the Mann's Grocery Stores. The prodigious Stradford Hotel, built by J.B. Stradford, was accompanied by haberdasheries, drug stores, cafés, barber shops and beauty salons, with a host of essential and luxury shops. In time, insurance companies were added to the Directory, and a skating rink was built.

J.B. (John Baptist) Stradford arrived in Tulsa only two years after Gurley, with his wife Augusta. The two men entered into a partnership dedicated to the district's development despite some differences of approach. They shared a mutual "distrust of white people,"[30] and accordingly, began the Greenwood practice of employing only their initials. For whites to address black men by their first name was considered a form of derision.

---

[30] Shomari Wills, Origins of Black Wall Street, Jan. 10, 2020, Investopedia – www.investopedia.com/insights/origins-black-wall-street/

Stradford

Stradford was the son of a former slave from Versailles, Kentucky, his father having been named Caesar by his owner. Befriended by the owner's daughter, Caesar eventually learned to read the Emancipation Proclamation that set him free. However, he first petitioned his master individually. On a journey from Kentucky to Ontario, he was set free and given the name of Stratford which he altered to Stradford. Working and saving, Caesar eventually obtained the liberty of his entire family, including his son J.B. The first-born son grew up to become a University of Indiana graduate, training as an attorney specializing in "social justice and racial solidarity to real estate."[31] In additional legal studies, Augusta and

---

[31] Black Wall Street, Centennial: Tulsa Pilgrimage, 2021, The Stradfords of Black Wall Street, Tulsa – www.blackwallstrett.org/jbstradford

J.B. were the only African Americans to enter and finish the law curriculum at Oberlin College.

Despite the relative safety of Greenwood during its development, Stradford was well aware that "in Oklahoma, it [was] not considered a crime for a mob to kill a negro."[32] He was an unconstrained voice against Jim Crow in Oklahoma, and typified the aggressive Greenwood response to racial insult. The occasional white visitor was astonished at the black lack of tolerance for remarks and epithets that would have elicited bowing and scraping in other communities, and by other men. Such an example was driven home when a white deliveryman hurled an offensive quip at Stradford on the street. Before he realized what had happened, Stradford had thrown him to the ground and proceeded to "straddle him and punch his face until it was bloody."[33] Not surprisingly, Stradford was charged with assault, but considering that the deliveryman had insulted him on hallowed ground for the African American, an acquittal was quickly handed down.

Stradford believed that a general success was to be achieved in a black community through the pooling of resources, collaborations in which fellow entrepreneurs were mutually supportive. As had Gurley, Stradford purchased large tracts of acreage in the northeast section

---

[32] Thomas F. Armstrong
[33] Shomari Wills

of Tulsa, subdivided them and sold them exclusively to African Americans. A number of other speculators followed suit. In the spirit of mutual support, businesses were serviced by colleagues from the community and their establishments instead of relying on resources from white Tulsa. One company, the Acme Brick Works, reaped the benefits of serving as the primary brick construction service in the district, and its work can be seen in nearly every structure of the 35-block commercial zone. While the African American money was being pooled, many in the district still worked for white employers, but did not allow any of their income to remain on the white side of the tracks. This form of "double-saving" grew the coffers silently and rapidly.

In a short time, Stradford's enterprises in the Greenwood District included two dozen rental properties worth a modern sum of two million. His mammoth hotel at 301 N. Greenwood, the largest black-owned hotel in America, stood as the "crown jewel,"[34] with 54 modern living rooms, a gambling hall, dining room, saloon, and pool hall. The Stradford Hotel was noted for its performances of jazz, along with the local Commodore Club. Greenwood was the town in which a young Count Basie first "encountered big-band jazz."[35] For a time, these

---

[34] Black Wall Street

[35] Black Past, Deep Greenwood (Tulsa) Oklahoma (1906-) – www.blackpast.org/African American-history/deep-greenwood-tulsa-1906/

celebrations could be held without repercussions. However, jazz was an almost embryonic art form in that era, and unsettling to the white population. Traditional Christians across the tracks labeled halls where such music was played as dens of iniquity, adding religious indignation to their resentment of a black community's superior wealth. Stradford was a marked man for his litigation against the railroad as well, as he fought for accommodations due the black traveler. He further "stirred the pot"[36] by railing against Jim Crow and in particular, segregation. His outrage against lynching of "peace loving"[37] neighbors by mobs was unconstrained.

The Stradford Hotel

Tulsa historian Scott Ellsworth, in *Death in the Promised Land*, recalls a time in which young Bill Williams asked his father why the family had moved from Mississippi to

36 Black Wall Street
37 Black Wall Street

Tulsa. John's response was simply, "I came out to the Promised Land."[38] John Wesley and Loula Tom Williams were wise to make the move, although as two of the earliest residents, little infrastructure was present by the time of their arrival at the turn of the century. The U.S. Census lists the couple as having been married five years. No black doctors had yet become established in Greenwood, and the hospital was not yet built. At the birth of their son William, the couple traveled to Hot Springs, Arkansas for the delivery.

John Williams had an extraordinary talent for machines of every sort, and for a time operated the chilling equipment for the Thompson Ice Cream Company. He was paid so well that he was eventually able to purchase the first automobile in Greenwood. Photos exist of the couple, with Bill in the back seat, sitting in their Chalmers Thirty Pony Tonneau. The thirty horsepower vehicle cost $1,600, the equivalent of $53,000 in modern currency, featuring a three-speed manual transmission and a top speed of 50 mph. Williams made all the repairs of the strange new contraption himself, and was so proficient at maintaining it that others started to bring their cars from Greenwood and the white section of town. Within a few years, John compiled a clientele list that enabled him to let go of his job at the ice cream company and open a garage.

---

[38] Carlos Moreno, The Victory of Greenwood: John and Loula Williams – www.thevictoryofgreenwood.com/2020/03/15/the-victory-of-greenwood-john-and-loula-greenwood/

At 420 E. Archer Street, in the middle of the financial action, Loula opened a confectionary where candied ice cream was offered and quit her teaching job. Adding an extensive soda fountain, the project was solely "Loula's baby,"[39] and a wildly popular one. The establishment became the central meeting place for the young, and it is said that in the intimate décor, "there were more proposals for marriage…than at any other place in the city."[40] As John's garage brought in handsome profits, he stayed busy constructing a three-story building to house apartments and office space to go along with the confectionary.

John and Loula Williams

Loula's successful venture left her with a taste for more, and the couple's next goal was to provide Greenwood

[39] Jennifer Latham.com, The Dreamland – www.jenniferlatham.com/?p=248

[40] Jennifer Latham.com

with a theater. In short order, their Empress Theatre opened in 1913 at 17 West 3rd Street. The Empress was no modest example, seating nearly 800 and featuring performances of stage musicals and vaudeville acts. She added a second theater that would become an iconic landmark even in Tulsa's present day, the Dreamland Theatre. In a case of ideal timing, the second theater paralleled the growth of the film industry. In addition to the infancy of Hollywood, black film companies abounded in the eastern half of the country, from Chicago to Florida. Closest to Tulsa was the Lincoln Motion Picture Company of Omaha. At the Dreamland, new movie-goers saw the much-anticipated film entitled *The Green-Eyed Monster*, with an all-black cast. The Williams fortune continued to grow with investments in other communities and John and Loula were to remain among the leading power couples of the community. The Dreamland was eventually burned to the ground in the coming race riots, but despite the insurance company's refusal to resurrect the theater, she had two others in Muskogee and Okmulgee.

Among the most important components of a community intending to chart its own course was a newspaper to serve the black community, defend their agenda, and resist injustice. Throughout the Midwest, South, and East, newspapers were in nearly all cases dominated by the

Republican Party's world view as the parties gradually switched the liberal-conservative positions. In Greenwood, *The Tulsa Star* emerged as the only "staunchly Democratic African American paper"[41] in the nation. In addition to its attention to local urges and exterior warnings, the *Star* was at all times promotive of the district's achievements. First on a weekly basis, then as a daily, the community's creation of hospitals, schools, theaters, and churches was trumpeted throughout the region.

The creator, editor and publisher of *The Tulsa Star* was Andrew Jackson Smitherman, who has been described as "spirited and bold…sometimes known to swim against the tide."[42]   In the beginning, Smitherman was wary of the district's "founding fathers," and in particular O.W. Gurley, whose authority seemed overblown. He was fond of referring to the town giant as "the King of Little Africa."[43] His early career was spent as a traveling agent and advertising manager for the distinctly Republican *Muskogee Cimeter*, published by William Henry Twine. Smitherman published his first paper four year later, *The Muskogee Star*, advocating "self-reliance"[44] for all black enclaves, and championing all black causes. Smitherman

[41] Oklahoma Historical Society the Gateway to Oklahoma History, Tulsa Star –
www.gateway.oklahomahistory.org/explore/collections/TULSA/

[42] Randy Krehbiel, Tulsa Race Massacre, Tulsa World – www.tulsaworld.com/tulsa-race-massacre-led-by-its-determined-editor-tulsa-star-challenged-racism-and-fought-against/article_ccbf6327-422c-5160-be57-c951c237d382.html

[43] Shomari Wills

[44] Oklahoma Historical Society

railed against racism in all of its manifestations. When
Republican news organizations claimed that black leaders
preferred Jim Crow transportation laws, the leader of the
Star shot back that if such were true, these supposed black
leaders were "ripe for a full coat of tar and feathers."[45]
The community's possession of such an important voice
was especially true as white Tulsa began to awaken to the
district's wealth. In 1914, a law was passed in the city that
prohibited any person from living on a block where three
quarters of the residency was of a different race,
maintaining racial purity in every district, especially the
predominantly white one.

Smitherman was at the least one of Greenwood's most
outspoken and occasionally colorful characters. Through
the years, many articles were printed about the editor
himself, uncommon in the industry. A few included
"Smitherman shoots at Flour Thief," "Smitherman and
His Family," "Smitherman and Dewey Riot," and
"Smitherman v. Rioters." In his fight for social justice,
Smitherman took the trouble to meet with the governor on
more than one occasion. His was the only paper to cover
Governor James B.A. Robertson's "inter-racial
conference."[46] In addition to his duties at the newspaper,
he was appointed Justice of the Peace as well.

---

[45] Randy Krehbiel

[46] Randy Krehbiel

When he lost everything in the 1921 race riot, Smitherman returned to run papers in Massachusetts and Buffalo, New York. An indictment based on white accusations that his paper ignited the riots hung over Smitherman's head for years, and he was under threat of immediate death if he ever returned to Tulsa. The Smitherman descendants, still residing in the Tulsa area, have been active in politics by coming to the forefront to discourage a public rally for President Donald Trump in the city. For all the grit in Smitherman's resistance to injustice, he was recalled as a warm family man, a quality that aroused his grandchildren to further his struggle. Those who knew their illustrious ancestor still remember him as a clever man filled with "wonderful ghost stories."[47]

The Greenwood District had every profession that one might find in a full-sized city, including an able group of attorneys accustomed to difficult times in white courtrooms. The most notable of these was Buck Colbert Franklin. Unlike most of his contemporaries, he did not migrate from the South, having been born in the town of Homer, Oklahoma. This placed him in the midst of Pickens County of the Chickasaw Nation, in the Indian Territory. He was named Buck in honor of his grandfather, although some believed that the elder

---

[47] Sean Kirst, In Buffalo, a hero journalist in Oklahoma found new life after Tulsa massacre, Buffalo News – www.buffalonews.com/news/local/in-buffalo-a-hero-journalist-found-new-life-after-tulsa-massacre/article_a9d2b6cb-0188-50d7-bref-04245-304a9df.html

Franklin escaped from his plantation and changed his name. As a young man, Franklin practiced law in Ardmore, Oklahoma, and not surprisingly, he often struggled to hold his ground within the white judicial system. He was once utterly silenced in a Louisiana courtroom solely on the basis of his race. In time, he married Mollie Parker and moved to the Greenwood District shortly before the riot. By that time, the district was "among the most affluent black communities in the nation."[48] He is most noted for representing several of the Tulsa survivors of the riot. Franklin's son, John Hope, was hailed for his reappraisal of the Civil War, and he assisted with the Supreme Court brief that resulted in *Brown v. Board of Education of Topeka.*

Franklin

Among the most essential components for such an enclave was public transportation, and Greenwood was blessed with the presence of Simon Berry, who devised a "nickel-a-ride" plan in a topless Model T. Ford. Further, he established a mass transit system of multiple buses so highly functional that the city of Tulsa eventually purchased it from him. The routes took riders all the way into Tulsa. He owned the Royal Hotel as well, and he regularly shuttled wealthy oil barons in his charter airline service. At the peak of his success, Berry is said to have earned over $500 per day. Tulsans will note that he created what is now known as Lincoln Park and built the first swimming pool in the city, along with other recreational facilities.

For medical service, the Lincoln Hospital came to serve the district admirably, in part due to the presence of Andrew C. Jackson, local physician and surgeon. The Mayo brothers, of Mayo Clinic fame, once asserted that Jackson was "the most able negro surgeon in America."[49] With such a reputation, he instilled a great sense of trust in all that he met, and he treated both races, an astonishing fact in the era.

To note the success of the district by the hands of so many "heavy hitters" brought together is not to say that the town was blithely unconcerned for its safety with white neighbors so near across the tracks. Other "Black Wall Streets" had come to grief, and the general community in Greenwood was well-aware of recent events elsewhere. On occasion, the district itself experienced individual cases of violence. In one instance, a white taxi driver was abducted and shot. The suspect was arrested and lynched, reminding the enclave of the "violent context"[50] in which they lived. Also fresh in the memory were past incidents in which successful black businessmen came to a bad end by doing too well. Only a few years before the establishment of Greenwood, two

---

[49] Hannibal B. Johnson, Author, Attorney, Consultant, The Ghosts of Greenwood Past, A Walk Down Black Wall Street, May 11, 2019 – www.hannibaljohnson.com/the-ghosts-of-greenwood-past-a-walk-down-black-wall-street

[50] Thomas F. Armstrong

Memphis grocers were lynched out of envy at their success. According to *The Guardian*, the two men "died on the altar of capitalism."[51] The message was clear: "black entrepreneurism has limits."[52]

Unrest

As the First World War began to reach its conclusion, East St. Louis, Illinois was the scene of one of the nation's worst race riots, a progression that followed a typical pattern. On February 4, 1917, 470 black workers arrived at the Aluminum Ore Company to replace striking white workers. After formal complaints of black worker migrations were filed, news broke of an attempted robbery of a white man perpetrated by a black man. White mobs formed and "rampaged through downtown,"[53] beating every black person who could be found. Trolleys and streetcars were stopped, and black riders were pulled out and severely beaten. As was typical in such events, Illinois' leaders called out the National Guard, and as it turned out, this was only the prelude to heightened violence erupting a few days later. Black homes were burned to the ground, and men, women, and children were beaten and shot to death.

On July 27, 1919, an African American teenager

---

[51] The Guardian, In 1921, A White Mob Burned Black Wall Street Down. We Still Feel That Legacy Today – www.guardian.com/comments is free/2020/jun/19/tulsa-1921-massacre-trump-violence-legacy/

[52] The Guardian

[53] Black Past, East St. Louis Race Riot, 1917 – www.blackpast.org/African American-history/east-st-louis race-riot-1917/

drowned in Lake Michigan after violating the unofficial segregation policy of Chicago's beaches. He was stoned by a group of white youths, bringing on what has been termed "The Red Summer." The police were called, but they refused to make an arrest, although the primary suspect was pointed out. That sparked a week of rioting between black and white Chicagoans in a South Side neighborhood near the stockyards, resulting in 15 whites and 23 blacks killed, as well as 500 people injured. An additional 1,000 black families lost their homes after they were torched by rioters. The violence was the culmination of rising tension as larger black migrations moved from the South to northern cities in search of work. Simultaneously, thousands of veterans returned home from Europe, only to find their factory jobs filled with Southern blacks and immigrants. The return of black veterans carried an added slight, as African American servicemen were excluded from the GI Bill.

In a period of financial instability, deep cultural prejudices ran rampant throughout the country. To exacerbate the situation, the KKK reinitiated a reign of terror in Southern cities and managed to work their way up to Chicago where the African American population in the city had grown to 100,000. As was usually the case, the state militia was called in, but President Woodrow Wilson blamed the black newcomers as "lawless instigators."[54]

The Klan inevitably arrived in Tulsa as well, where a success story such as Greenwood was a magnet for the organization's racist violence, but before the 1921 riot, the rigidity of segregation helped the renowned entrepreneurial center of Greenwood avoid the social catastrophes exploding in other cities. The financial sector bloomed quickly with few peripheral crises. The influx of new black settlers that followed required an expansion of facilities including service businesses, schools, and entertainment centers. By 1920, black settlers had established 50 black communities scattered throughout the state of Oklahoma.

Hannibal Johnson, a Tulsa based historian, noted ironically that the indignities of Jim Crow created the Greenwood model as "an economy born of necessity." Black Americans fully understood that they could not thrive in a multiracial competition when even President Warren G. Harding's "passive racism"[55] underscored his inability to mount a response to the unrest in 1921.

The death knell for Black Wall Street began on Memorial Day, May 31, 1921. Around or after 4:00 p.m. that day, a clerk at Renberg's clothing store on the first

[54] History.com, The Red Summer of 1919 – www.history.com/black-history/chicago-race-riot0of-1919

[55] James Lutzweiler, Review of Hannibal Johnson's Black Wall Street: From Riot to Renaissance in Tulsa's Historic Greenwood District, the *Southwestern Historical Quarterly* Vol. 103, No. 4, Texas State Historical Association

floor of the Drexel Building in Tulsa heard a woman scream. Turning in the direction of the scream, he saw a young black man running from the building. Going to the elevator, the clerk found the white elevator operator, 17-year-old Sarah Page, crying and distraught. The clerk concluded that she had been assaulted by the black man he saw running a few moments earlier and called the police.

Those facts are just about the only things people agree on when it comes to the riot in Tulsa in 1921. By the time the unrest ended, an unknown number of Tulsa's black citizens were dead, over 800 people were injured, and what had been the wealthiest black community in the United States had been laid to waste.

In the days after the riot, a group formed to work on rebuilding the Greenwood neighborhood, which had been all but destroyed. The former mayor of Tulsa, Judge J. Martin, declared, "Tulsa can only redeem herself from the country-wide shame and humiliation into which she is today plunged by complete restitution and rehabilition of the destroyed black belt. The rest of the United States must know that the real citizenship of Tulsa weeps at this unspeakable crime and will make good the damage, so far as it can be done, to the last penny."

However, financial assistance would be slow in coming, a jury would find that black mobs were responsible for the damage, and not a single person was ever convicted as a result of the riot. Indeed, given that racist violence directed at blacks was the norm in the Jim Crow South, and accusations of black teens or adults violating young white girls were often accepted without evidence, people barely batted an eye at the damage wrought by the riot, which would remain largely overlooked for almost 70 years. Only in the last two decades have Oklahomans reckoned with this shameful episode in their history.

A picture taken during the riot

A picture taken during the riot on Archer and Greenwood

Among the many embarrassments of a feeble and corrupt Harding presidency, Johnson suggests that there should have been at the least a telegram sent to the effect of "What in hell is going on in Tulsa?"[56] Warren's typical failure to address such painful dramas in his own country should have been a greater point of embarrassment than the Teapot Dome or revelations of his mistress. James Lutzweiler suggested that although Johnson's proximity to the community offers a richness of detail and deep feeling, the author "may have had more Baptist history than business history"[57] in his approach. All in all,

---

[56] James Lutzweiler

Johnson was accurate in his view that such a circumstance called for black isolation in the realm of business in the absence of an honest game.

Greenwood's Legacy

Anticipating the model of successful isolation played out by black entrepreneurs in places like Greenwood would have been perfectly understandable had white America been paying attention. All major black leaders, including W.E.B. Du Bois, Booker T. Washington, and Marcus Garvey, exhorted their people to build their own businesses free of white entanglement. It was a valid hope that to demonstrate self-leadership would enhance racial confidence, create trust outside the black community, and keep the black dollar in the black family where it was most needed. To do otherwise was to prolong the suffering caused by racial bias in lending, a dearth of property rights, an unwilling insurance industry, scant police protection, and little say in governmental matters. To own and self-promote was only the model, and its fulfillment required a collective of trusting black patrons who fell in with the idea that to accept lesser citizenship would leave them vulnerable in perpetuity.

The isolationist, mutually collaborative business model adopted by Greenwood was based on the idea that a

---

[57] James Lutzweiler

neglected race should "take advantage of the disadvantage."[58] In this contrarian view of segregation, an academic version of picking up one's marbles and going home, self-rule and mutual assistance produced the desired effect. A concentration of black entrepreneurs in the Greenwood district, with strongly marked borders, exploited a strong black market, as leaders claimed it would. It mobilized a community of black purchasers to support home-grown businesses, fulfilling Booker T. Washington's dream of "an independent black economy."[59] It cemented that success by guaranteeing that no desirable product was absent. It was understood that to take away one jewelry store or beauty shop would cause the clientele to search for it elsewhere. That business being lost, the district would have risked double jeopardy, as the wayward purchaser would be introduced into a new and alien shopping district. To make the enterprise airtight, no attraction could be absent. In terms of logistics and concentration of population, Greenwood enhanced "the level of enterprise"[60] by presenting an absolute palette and eliminating the need to consider traveling outside the district. The 35 blocks centered around Greenwood and Archer, with its self-contained offering, proved that while social integration may be good for people and nations,

---

[58] Robert L. Boyd, Black Enterprise in the Retail Trade During the Early 20th Century, *Sociological Focus,* Vol. 34 No. 3 (August 2001), Taylor & Francis Ltd.

[59] Robert L. Boyd

[60] Robert L. Boyd

commercial segregation is good for business in a disadvantaged collective. This has proven to be even more true in economic recessions, during which the pressure increases for being self-employed. The relative size of the ethnic population was a plus for Greenwood. For the developmental stage, the evil of "leaking money" was avoided, a financial malady in which the community dollars "wake up in the morning in the African community, but…go to sleep at night in the white community."[61] Such a strategy was referred to as the "economic detour theory,"[62] one that keeps dollars at home, important in the amassing of centralized wealth. However, it is suggested by some economic historians that clinging to this strategy eventually causes problems for collective triumph if not taken to the larger world for eventual investment. Had the infamous race riots not occurred, how long the model would have sustained itself is unclear.

For Greenwood's purposes, however, self-help was the central requirement. The isolation model had been used successfully in the past by immigrants building small businesses in one sector, such as the Italian garment industry. Equally profitable was the food industry or other collectives. They all stayed close to home and employed

---

[61] Roy L. Brooks, Integration or Separation? A Strategy for Racial Equality, Ch. 17, *Integration within the Community*, Harvard University Press

[62] Robert L. Boyd

their neighborhood's families to keep profit from escaping. They realized that to compete as a slighted player, an economic base cannot be forged without vulnerability and frailty of fortune. For Greenwood, the lesson was well-earned and brilliantly applied, with self-help, self-production, and self-management providing the perfect "antidote"[63] to poverty. It was accomplished not through the mega-corporation built of outside influences, but by the family business sustained by the district's own labor force.

As for the deeper, abiding reasons for Greenwood's downfall, let loose by a trigger event, the downside of isolation may have been played out by the district's success. The lasting residue was indeed real, as black submission of patents "plunged"[64] in the following years throughout the nation. By allowing blacks to take over the business reins, the white population lost the black dependence on which it relied for financial viability, either by slaves or emancipated workers. Chris M. Messer offers four points of collective behavior in humans that make up the process of rebellion. First, people are vulnerable to destructive behavior when "confronted with an ambiguous situation."[65] Black independence certainly

---

[63] Roy L. Brooks

[64] Paul Krugman, Tulsa and the Many Sins of Racism, New York Times, June 18, 2020 –
www.nytimes.com/2020/06/18/opinion/tulsa-racism.html

[65] Chris M. Messer, The Tulsa Race Riot of 1921: Toward an Integrative Theory of Collective Violence, *Journal of Social History*,
Oxford University Press

fulfilled that criteria. Paralleling that is the assumption that in such a setting, people look to others around them for behavioral guidance. When they see few negative consequences, they are likely to arouse more newly "emergent"[66] group norms than they might have in times of conventional circumstances. Separate from the "absolute deprivation" of minorities at a disadvantage, the white mob of Tulsa was overwhelmed with "relative deprivation" after watching yesterday's slaves wear "satin dresses and diamonds…silk shirts and gold chains."[67] Residents enjoying the good life were simultaneously aware of Tulsa's seething tension, one observing "That resentment in Tulsa was so intense."[68] White Tulsa was suddenly living a slice of the black experience, the difference being that white society had kept the majority of numbers and weaponry with which to strike back.

The Greenwood example was admirably rebuilt in large measure, but the tightness of the community was never restored. One may suggest that with increasing integration in the United States, such a guarded economy was no longer necessary. Some may differ, asserting that such a phenomenon is once again needed. John W. Rogers, the grandson of J.B. Stradford and Chairman of Aerial Investments, has carried on the tradition of supporting a

---

[66] Chris M. Messer

[67] Meagan Day, The History of the Tulsa Massacre that Destroyed America's Wealthiest Black Neighborhood, *Timeline*, Sept. 21, 2016 – www.timeline.com/history-tulsa-face-massacre-a92bb2356a69

[68] Meagan Day

black economy. He claims that among other assets, the upside of Greenwood proves that "when we are left to ourselves and don't have a knee to our neck, we can achieve extraordinary things."[69] Rogers founded the first black-owned Mutual fund company and his mother Jewel became the first African American to graduate from the School of Law at the University of Chicago. President Eisenhower appointed her as U.S. District Attorney for northern Illinois, and she was the first black woman in history to argue a case before the Supreme Court of the United States. That J.B. Stradford would have been inordinately proud of his descendant's achievements seems likely, and also that he would not be in the least surprised.

Rogers laments that the Greenwood money never got its chance to be compounded over a lengthy period of time. The district's families made good use of their success, but did not accrue it with the intent to "reinvest, diversify, or expand."[70] There might have come a time in which such actions were less problematic in the modern civil rights era. In time, the black economy needed to try its wings in the larger world. However, as a result of Greenwood's destruction, perpetual generational wealth was not created in the way it might have been. He adds in response to white perceptions of the Greenwood history that all too

____

[69] Forbes
[70] Forbes

often the white citizen does not connect bigotry to economic exploitation. They often deplore prejudice and the violence that attends it, "but have tolerated or ignored economic injustice"[71] at the same time.

In the modern era, black wealth in what was Tulsa's Greenwood District has remained "relatively flat"[72] while the white economy soars. The wealth gap in the U.S. widens, and the cultural point emphasized by the Greenwood experiment fades into a largely untaught history. In a literal sense, the "Black Wall Street" carried only a minute fraction of the volume enjoyed by the district in New York. Washington's term was always intended as a symbolic tribute, a depiction of intelligent, collaborative investment in entrepreneurship and personal drive in a race not originally thought to possess it.

Early white America, and elements of the present white culture were and continue to be in error. The model for ethnic wealth exists, and has been proven in fact over fantasy. The Greenwood experiment debunked every existing stereotype for keeping black business under heel. Such an exposure of old myths was not only important for the white business world to witness but also a demonstration of it was needed for subsequent generations of black entrepreneurs. Their professional ancestors

---

[71] Forbes

[72] Yahoo Finance, Why Black Wealth Has Stayed Relatively Flat Since the Tulsa Massacre - www.finance.yahoo.com/news/why-black-wwealth-has-stayed-rlatively-flat-sincetulsa-0massacre-150041181.html

experienced the continent's inherent cultural suppression, and had the old South's mythology lodged in their collective mindset, to be exported anywhere a black citizen might reside. Left unchallenged, the poison of surrender spread to future generations encountering more subtle tactics of the same curse. Greenwood boosted black confidence as an immovable historical fact, and handed down a model for success. The blueprint for working it is currently in the hands of any African American with the ideas and determination with which to impel its manifestation.

  In the typical business model of the Greenwood District, the African American "out-whited" the white businessman. That the Greenwood District's time had not yet come is likely incorrect. Its citizens were ready, willing, and up to the task of creating a civic jewel on the prairie. More apt is that the time of fending off such a degree of resistance had not yet come. Historians to psychiatrists suggest that by the era of Greenwood's existence, the white process of acceptance had begun to run its course over far too short a time span. White sensitivities could not yet truly stand up under the pressure of possession jealousy or unfamiliar personal liberties among the slave class. Some might wonder if the time has come even in the present day for blacks to succeed without fear.

Diaries and other testimonial avenues have created interesting stories as we identify the last citizens of Greenwood still alive. Olivia Hooker, considered to be the oldest, basks in the recollection that the district "was a neighborhood where you could be treated with respect."[73] Hooker became the first black woman to join the United States Coast Guard. Her best competitor for the title is Hal Singer. On the day of Greenwood's destruction, he was hurried onto a train for Kansas City at 18 months of age. At the age of 98 in 2018, he had gone on to be a noted professional jazz saxophonist and band leader.

Of the original group of black towns created in the Oklahoma Territory, 13 exist in the present day. Most are situated in a ring around the city of Tulsa. Clearview was established in Okfuskee County, and by the second Census of the 20th century housed 48 citizens. Vernon can be found in the southwestern portion of McIntosh County, and was established four years after statehood. The population is unknown. Langston, created by Edwin McCabe, houses Langston University, and was home to 1,724 by the year of 2010. Brooksville is located in Pottawatomie County to the southwest of Tecumseh. Established somewhat earlier, it was originally named Sewell for a white doctor who owned much of the surrounding lands. Most residents departed through the

[73] NPR, Code Switch, Meet the Last Surviving Witness to the Tulsa Race Riot of 1921 –
www.npr.org/section/codeswitch/2018/05/31/615546965/meet-the-last-surviving-witnesws-to-the-tulsa-race-riot-of-1921

early century, but the town survived, boasting 63 residents. Grayson was established in southeastern Okmulgee County barely after the turn of the century. It was named for Chief George W. Grayson and it once featured five general stores, two blacksmiths, two drug stores, a physician, and a cotton gin. At the turn of the twenty-first century, the African American percentage was 64.1%, 9.8% white and 9.8% Native American. It built two schools, two churches, and a convention center that is employed for voting. Lima was created in Seminole County two years prior and Seminoles and their freedmen blacks occupied the town. Never incorporated, the population has fallen under 270. Boley, once the most successful in the lineage leading up to Greenwood, housed many businesses including two banks, three cotton gins, and two colleges. The 2010 Census lists the population as 1,184. Tatums appeared early in the process, and was in the midst of numerous oil wells on an extensive field, in addition to a sawmill and hotel. The population is 151. Rentiesville stands only a few miles from Muskogee, home to a famous blues man and band leader, D.C. Minner. After a Civil War battle that occurred there, the town was called "the Gettysburg of the West."[74]

Among those who documented the tragedy that befell

---

[74] Tulsa World.com, Gallery: The 13 Historic all black towns that remain in Oklahoma, Feb. 26, 2020 –
www.tulsaworld.com/news/state-and-regional/gallery-the-13-historic-all-black-touwns-that-remain-in
Oklahoma/collection_7dicl7b5d-662c-54a0-a072-bc56afdf6756756.html#1

Greenwood on film, were both amateur and professional documentaries that have left us visual accounts of the revival. Reverend Harold Mose Anderson, for example, was "fascinated by the movies."[75] Accordingly, he bought a home movie camera and wandered the streets of Tulsa in the years following the Second World War. The result has been *Harold Anderson's Black Wall Street Film*, with footage captured between 1948-1952 and preserved by the National Museum of American History's Archives Center. His days of roaming the avenues and residential streets of the old district documents everyday life in a resurrected Greenwood after growing up with the stories and observing the town's rebirth. As a whimsical example of old nostalgia for the original community, a board game has been created entitled *Black Wall Street*, the African American answer to *Monopoly*. The concept of the game, however, is no pure joke, but expertly teaches a young player about "both history and financial literacy."[76]

A documentary entitled *Black Wall Street* claims expanded statistics from those found in other sources. A total of 600 businesses are said to have resided within a 36 square block area, and in general, a dollar spent in Greenwood circulated over 100 times before it reached a white district. The documentary cites the number of those

[75] Wendy Shay, contributions by Patricia Sanders, Black Wall Street on Film: A Story of Revival and Renewal, *National Museum of American History*, Feb. 24, 2017 – www.americanhistory.si.edu/blog/black-wall-street

[76] Kimberly C. Ellis, Ph.D., It's Time We All Learned About Black Wall Street and the Tulsa Massacre – dictionary.com/e/black-wall-street-tulsa-massacre

holding a Ph.D. who resided in the area, and a reminder that in the era of 1920s, physicians owned medical schools. The population is listed as 15,000, and of all the principles of business within the enclave, the most appreciated word was "nepotism…the one word they truly believed in."[77]

External international views have always abounded as alien systems analyze struggle for civil rights in the United States. The Marxist concept dispenses much blame for America's allegedly faulty economic system, ignoring the racial fracturing committed from the beginning, an opinion shared with much of Europe. In recounting historical reality, however, proponents of the communist system make a few salient points, such as white society's continued dependence on black labor well into the 19th century, and in certain cases, beyond. Elmer T. Allison asserts that "the foundation on which its economic, civil, and moral superstructure is built – [is] chattel slavery."[78] He adds that with the Jim Crow laws that reinserted white domination into law, the emancipation story was rendered all but fictitious, especially for the South. The plantation patriarch wanted it to remain the way it was before and after the Civil War, and he intended to have it one way or the other. He labels capitalist society as a "conspiracy

---

[77] Black Wall Street, Tulsa, Oklahoma, Culture, Race, and Economy – aalb.albc.com/tc/topic/1419-black-wall-street-in-tulsa-oklahoma

[78] Elmer T. Allison, The Economic Basis of the Tulsa Race Riot – www.marxisthistory.org/history/usa/parties/cpusa/192106/18-allison-tulsa-basis.pdf

against the negro,"[79] the same as any "pogrom-ridden nation against the Jews."[80] In the West, however, most simply ascribe the ongoing crisis to racism.

James O. Goodwin, owner of the weekly paper, *The Oklahoma Eagle*, is connected to Greenwood through his grandfather, who worked for Smitherman's *Tulsa Star*. *The Eagle* was a long-lived paper that rose from the ashes of the *Star*, and it remained for some time in the hands of his father. When it was time, his retirement led to a summons for James to take over. When he expressed doubt due to considering other plans, his father simply said, "Come home, or I'm going to give away the paper."[81] Goodwin is quick to caution that what the black collective achieved was neither an exceptional fluke stumbled upon by an unthinking people, nor was it such a rare exception at all. Until it was brutally halted, Greenwood's quest for economic equality was accomplished in the sight of a white majority that feared it might be replicated in the future. Put simply, Black Wall Street was not operating in a strange new manner, but simply doing business the way other segments of segregated societies were doing business.

Thus, as a moniker for the historical district, America's

---

[79] Elmer T. Allison

[80] Elmer T. Allison

[81] Kurtis Lee, This Newspaper Has Never Forgotten the 1921 Tulsa Race Massacre - and its Fight Continues, Workers World, LA Times – www.workers.org/1000/06/49482

"Black Main Street" might have been a more accurate metaphor than Washington's term, and Goodwin takes his cue from this loftier vision. He cites a higher purpose in the recognition of Greenwood's feat, one that elevates the question above racial competition, but remains all about racial equality: "The significant thing about Greenwood is that it was not just a black thing. It was quintessential America."[82]

Online Resources

<u>Other books about 20th century history by Charles River Editors</u>

<u>Other books about the Tulsa race riot on Amazon</u>

Bibliography

Allison, Elmer T., The Economic Basis of the Tulsa Race Riot – www.marxisthistory.org/history/usa/prties/cpusa/1921/06/18-allison-tulsa-basis

Armstrong, Thomas F., Review of Scott Ellsworth's Death in a Promised Land, the Tulsa Race Riot of 1921, Reviews in American History Vol. 11 no. 1 (March1983) Johns Hopkins University Press

Black Past, Edward P. McCabe (1850-1920) – www.blackpast.org/African American-history/maccabe-

---

[82] Antoine Gara

edwin-p-1850-1920/

Black Past, Deep Greenwood (Tulsa) Oklahoma (1906-) – www.blackpast.org/African American-history/deep-greenwood-tula-ok-1906/

Black Wall Street, Centennial: Tulsa Pilgrimage, 2021, The Stradfords of Black Wall Street, Tulsa – www.blackwallstrett.org/jbstradford

Black Wall Street, Tulsa, Oklahoma, Culture, Race, and Economy – www.aalbc.com/tc/topic/1419-black-wall-street-in-tulsa-oklahoma/

Bowyer, Jerry, Tulsa Massacre: The Loser Class vs. Black Entrepreneurs, Townhall Finance, June 23, 2020 – www.finance.townhall.com/columnists/jerrybowyer/2020/06/23/tulsa-massacre-the-loser-class-vs-black-entrepreneurs-n2571165

Clark, Alexis Tulsa's "Black Wall Street" Flourished as a Self-Contained Hub in Early 1900s, History.com – www.history.com/news/black-wall-street-tulsa-race-massacre

Ellis, Kimberly C., Ph.D., It's Time We All Learned About Black Wall Street and the Tulsa Massacre – www.dictionary.com/e/black-wall-street-tulsa-massacre/

Gara, Antoine, The Bezos of Black Wall Street, Forbes –

www.forbes.com/peter/antoinegara/2020/06/18the-bezos-of-black-wall-street-tulsa-race-riots-1921/#5b37f7c7f321

Gilmore Glenda, Jumpin' Jim Crow: Southern Politics from Civil War to Civil Rights, Department of African American Studies, Yale University – www.afamstudies.yale.edu/publications/jumpin'-him-crow-Southern-politics-civil-war-civil-rights

Harriot, Michael, The Other Black Wall Streets, The Root – www.theroot.com, the-other-black-wall-streets-1823010812

History.com, The Trail of Tears, Feb. 21, 2020 – www.history.com/topics/native-american-history/trail-of-tears

History.com, The Red Summer of 1919 – www.history.com/black-history/chicago-race-riot0of-1919

Kirst, Sean, In Buffalo, a hero journalist in Oklahoma found new life after Tulsa massacre, Buffalo News – www.buffalonews.com/news/local/in-buffalo-a-hero-journalist-found-new-life-after-tulsa-massacre/article_a9d2b6cb-0188-50d7-bref-04245-304a9df.html

Johnson, Hannibal B., Author, Attorney, Consultant, The Ghosts of Greenwood Past, A Walk Down Black Wall

Street, May 11, 2019 – www.hannibaljohnson.com/the-ghosts-of-greenwood-past-a-walk-down-black-wall-street

Krehbiel, Randy Tulsa Race Massacre, Tulsa World – www.tulsaworld.com/tulsa-race-massacre-led-by-its-determined-editor-tulsa-star-challenged-racism-and-fought-against/article_ccbf6327-422c-5160-be57-c951c237d382.html

Krugman, Paul Tulsa and the Many Sins of Racism, New York Times, June 18, 2020 – www.nytimes.com/2020/06/18/opinion/tulsa-racism.html

Lee, Kurtis, This Newspaper Has Never Forgotten the 1921 Tulsa Race Massacre – and Its Fight Continues – Workers World, LA Times, Mary 22, 2020 – www.workers.org/2000/06/49482

Lutzweiler, James, Review of Hannibal Johnson's Black Wall Street: From Riot to Renaissance in Tulsa's Historic Greenwood District, the Southwestern Historical Quarterly Vol. 103, No. 4, Texas State Historical Association

Maloney, Thomas N., University of Utah, African Americans in the 20th Century, E.H. Net – www.eh.net/encyclopedia/African Americans-in-the-20th-century

Moreno, Carlos, The Victory of Greenwood: John and

Loula Williams –
www.thevictoryofgreenwood.com/2020/03/15/the-victory-of-greenwood-john-and-loula-greenwood/

Oklahoma Historical Society, All-Black Town –
www.oklahomahistory.org/publications/end/entry-php?entry=AL009

Oklahoma Historical Society, Greenwood District –
www.okhistory.org/publications/enc/entry.php?entry=GR024

Oklahoma Historical Society, Ku Klux Klan-
www.okhistory.org/publications/enc/entry.php?entry=KU001

Oklahoma Historical Society, Senate Bill One –
okhistory.com/publications/enc/entry/php?entry=SE017

Roberts, Alaina E., Assistant Professor, University of Pittsburgh, Commemorating the Tulsa Massacre: A Search for Identity and Historical Complexity, June 4, 2020 – www.ncph.org/history-at-work/commemorating-tulsa-massacre/

Savage, William W. Jr., History is Clear: Alfalfa Bill Murray was a Terrible Bigot, Thursday, June 18, 2020, Non Doc.com – www.nondoc.com/2020/06/18/alfalfa-bill-murray-was-a-terrible-bigot/

Shay, Wendy, contributions by Patricia Sanders, Black Wall Street on Film: A Story of Revival and Renewal, National Museum of American History, Feb. 24, 2017 – www.americanhistory.si.edu/blog/black-wall-street

Smith, Ryan P., How Native American Slaveholders Complicate the Trail of Tears Narrative, Smithsonian Magazine –

Sean Kirst, In Buffalo, a hero journalist in Oklahoma found new life after Tulsa massacre, Buffalo News – www.buffalonews.com/news/local/in-buffalo-a-hero-journalist-found-new-life-after-tulsa-massacre/article_a9d2b6cb-0188-50d7-bref-04245-304a9df.html

The Guardian, In 1921, A White Mob Burned Black Wall Street Down, We Still Feel That Legacy Today – www.guardian.com/commentsisfree/2020/jun/19/tulsa-1921-massacre-trump-violence-legacy/

Tulsa World.com, Gallery: The 13 Historic all black towns that remain in Oklahoma, Feb. 26, 2020 – www.tulsaworld.com/news/state-and-regional/gallery-the-13-historic-all-black-touwns-that-remain-in Oklahoma/collection_7dicl7b5d-662c-54a0-a072-bc56afdf6756756.html#1

Wills, Shomari, Origins of Black Wall Street,

Investopedia, January 10, 2020 –
www.investopedia.com/insights/origins-black-all-street/

   Yahoo Finance, Why Black Wealth Has Stayed
Relatively Flat Since the Tulsa Massacre -
www.finance.yahoo.com/news/why-black-wwealth-has-
stayed-rlatively-flat-sincetulsa-0massacre-
150041181.html

Free Books by Charles River Editors

We have brand new titles available for free most days of the week. To see which of our titles are currently free, [click on this link](#).

Discounted Books by Charles River Editors

We have titles at a discount price of just 99 cents everyday. To see which of our titles are currently 99 cents, click on this link.